COWS DON'T GIVE MILK & OTHER SHORT STORIES

Small Stories - Big Lessons

NIKHIL PANSE

Made with ❤ on the Notion Press Platform
www.notionpress.com

For Shreya

11th Nov 22

Preface

This book began as a personal project—a collection of stories I started compiling for my daughter for her thirteenth birthday. I wanted her to have something she could return to, not just now, but at different points in her life. Something that could comfort, guide, or ground her, especially when I might not be around. And as I collected and re-read these stories, I realized they aren't just for her—they're for all of us.

What we read has a deep impact on how we think, feel, and grow. Stories open our minds, spark our creativity, and often help us see the world differently. Sometimes, a simple story can offer comfort when we're feeling low, perspective when we're unsure, or a gentle nudge when we're stuck. They may not always give answers, but they often help us ask the right questions.

This is a collection of short stories or fables or parables or anecdotes or whatever you choose them to be. These stories have been adapted/modified to enhance clarity, engagement, and relevance for today's reader. Some of them are true, some are said to be true, and some are simply timeless narratives passed through generations.

I've read them many times over, and I've always come away with something new. Some stories are deeply inspiring, showing what's possible with grit and determination. Others are quiet, philosophical and thought provoking. These stories aren't preachy. They make you think and hit differently as you grow or go through different situations in life.

Stories like these don't age. You can visit them again and again—on a sad day, a joyful one, when you feel lost, when you lose hope or even when you feel like the boss of the world. Whatever the moment, you'll find something to hold on to. And that's why I've put this book together—for Shreya, and for all of us.

If you're seeking a little calm in the chaos, a glimmer of hope, some quiet encouragement, or a nudge of motivation—this book is for you.

Whether you're chasing a dream, dodging a dilemma, battling the unbeatable or just need a story to feel a bit more like yourself, this book is for you.

Happy reading.

Cheers

Dr. Nikhil Panse
Professor of Plastic Surgery

I'd love to hear your thoughts, reflections, or even your favourite story from the book. This book is a conversation—feel free to write back @ drnpanse@gmail.com

Contents

Who is Packing Your Parachute?

Air Commodore Vishal was a jet pilot. On a combat mission, his fighter plane was hit by a missile. He ejected just in time and parachuted safely to the ground. His courage and quick thinking won him praise and admiration from all quarters.

Five years later, Vishal was sitting with his wife in a quiet corner of a restaurant. As they talked, a man from another table walked up to him. "You're Captain Vishal! You flew jet fighters. You were shot down!" the man said, smiling.

Vishal was taken aback. "How do you know that?" he asked, his curiosity piqued.

"I packed your parachute," the man replied, still smiling.

Vishal froze for a moment, his mind racing. A wave of gratitude swept over him. He realized that if the parachute hadn't worked perfectly that day, he wouldn't be alive to share this moment.

That night, Vishal lay in bed, unable to sleep. His thoughts kept returning to that man. How many times might he have passed by him without even acknowledging his presence? A simple "Good morning" or "How are you?" would have been enough. But he hadn't.

Vishal had been a fighter pilot—a hero in the skies. But that man, a safety worker who packed parachutes, was the one who had truly saved his life.

Life often gives us people who silently provide the support we need—the parachutes that carry us through tough times. These parachutes come in many forms—physical, mental, emotional, spiritual, and financial. When challenges strike, we rely on them to bring us back to safety.

But how often do we stop to acknowledge those who quietly pack our parachutes? Perhaps it's time to reflect and show gratitude to those who help us land safely when life throws us into freefall. Sometimes in the daily challenges that life gives us, we miss what is important. So, who is packing your parachute?

———◆◆———

Narrative Context: This story is adapted from & inspired by a real-life account shared by Charles Plumb, a former U.S. Navy jet pilot, who often recounts his experience of meeting the man who packed his parachute.

The Bag of Cookies

Imagine yourself at a bustling airport, waiting for your flight. You pass by a kiosk selling cookies, and after a moment's thought, you buy a box. You tuck it into your travel bag and begin scanning the area for an empty seat. Finally, you spot one next to a quiet-looking gentleman and settle down, ready to enjoy your cookies.

As you reach into your bag and open the box, you notice something strange. The man besides you watches closely, his eyes following your hand as you pick up a cookie. Before you can process this, he does something even more surprising—he calmly reaches over, takes one of your cookies, and eats it!

You freeze. Did that really just happen? Words fail you. But as you take another cookie, he follows suit, taking one as well. For every cookie you eat, he takes one too. Your mind races. Who does that? Crazy? Rude? Unbelievable! Yet, you say nothing, trying to maintain your composure.

The cookies disappear quickly, and soon, there's just one left. Before you can reach for it, the man picks it up. But instead of eating it, he breaks it in half and offers you one piece. He smiles gently, eats his half, and without saying a word, gets up and walks away.

You sit there, stunned. Did that really happen? You're still hungry and confused, so you head back to the kiosk and buy another box of cookies. When you return to your seat and begin opening the new box, something catches your eye.

There, at the bottom of your bag, is your original box of cookies—still unopened!

A wave of realization washes over you. You had been eating the other man's cookies all along. And yet, he had shared them with you without a hint of annoyance.

Your perception of him shifts instantly. Words like kind, patient, and generous replace crazy, rude, unbelievable! You have just experienced a profound "paradigm shift".

Things aren't always what they seem. Sometimes, a different perspective can change everything. Life often presents multiple angles to a situation—your side, my side, and the truth. And sometimes, it takes a simple box of cookies to make you see things differently.

———❖❖———

Narrative Context: This story is adapted from "The Cookie Thief" by Valerie Cox, a popular short story often shared as a reflection on shifting perspectives and assumptions.

The Pocket Watch

The telephone rang. Jack answered. It was his mother. "Mr. Smith died last night," she said softly. "The funeral is on Wednesday."

Memories flooded Jack's mind like an old newsreel. His childhood came rushing back—days spent at Mr. Smith's house, learning and laughing.

"Jack, did you hear me?" his mother asked, pulling him back to the present.

"Sorry, Mom. Yes, I heard you," Jack said, his voice distant. "I haven't thought about him in so long. I honestly thought he passed away years ago."

"Well, he never forgot you," she said gently. "Every time I saw him, he'd ask about you. He'd talk about the days you spent on 'his side of the fence,' as he liked to say."

"I loved that old house," Jack murmured, a hint of a smile tugging at the corners of his lips.

"After your father died, Mr. Smith stepped in. He made sure you had a man's influence in your life," she reminded him softly.

"He's the one who taught me carpentry," Jack said, his voice filled with quiet gratitude. "I wouldn't be in this business if it weren't for him. He taught me things that really mattered." He paused for a moment. "I'll be there for the funeral, Mom."

As busy as he was, Jack kept his promise. He caught the next flight home.

Mr. Smith's funeral was small and quiet. He had no children, and most of his family had passed away. The evening before his return flight, Jack and his mother visited the old house next door.

Jack stood in the doorway, pausing for a moment. Stepping inside felt like stepping back in time. The house looked exactly as he remembered. Every creak in the floor, every piece of furniture, and every picture on the wall was a reminder of the past.

But something was missing.

Jack's eyes scanned the familiar room and stopped. "The box is gone," he murmured.

"What box?" his mother asked, puzzled.

"There was a small gold box he kept on top of his desk. I must have asked him a thousand times what was inside," Jack said, his voice trailing off. "All he'd ever say was, 'The thing I value most.'"

But now, it was gone. Everything else was exactly as it had been, except for the box. Jack figured someone from Mr. Smith's family had taken it.

"Now, I'll never know what was inside," Jack sighed. "I'd better get some sleep. I have an early flight tomorrow."

Two weeks passed. Life resumed its usual pace. One evening, as Jack returned home from work, he found a note in his mailbox.

"Signature required for a package. Please collect it from the post office within three days."

The next morning, Jack went to retrieve the package. It was small and looked like it had been mailed a hundred years ago. The handwriting was faint, but the return address caught his eye.

"Mr. Paul Smith."

Jack's heart pounded. He took the package to his car, ripped it open, and there it was—the gold box. Inside was a letter, and taped to the note was a small key.

Jack's hands trembled as he read the words:

"Upon my death, please forward this box and its contents to Jack Bennett. It's the thing I valued most in my life."

With a racing heart and tears in his eyes, Jack carefully unlocked the box.

Inside, he found a stunning gold pocket watch. The craftsmanship was flawless. His fingers traced the delicate etching on the cover before gently opening it.

Engraved inside were the words:

"Jack, Thanks for your time!—Paul Smith."

Jack's throat tightened. The thing Mr. Smith had valued most wasn't an object. It was the time they had spent together.

Jack held the watch close for a moment, his mind racing with memories. Then, without hesitation, he pulled out his phone and called his office.

"Sophia, I need to clear my schedule for the next two days," he said.

"Why?" Sophia asked, surprised.

"I need some time to spend with the people I love and care for," Jack replied softly.

After a pause, he added, "Oh, by the way, Sophia... thanks for your time." "Life is not measured by the number of breaths we take but by the moments that take our breath away." Think about this.

———— ❖❖ ————

Narrative Context: This story is adapted from the widely shared inspirational story "The Gold Box" by an unknown author and shared across social media platforms.

The Doll's Journey

When he was 40, Franz Kafka, the renowned Bohemian novelist and short story writer, was strolling through Steglitz Park in Berlin. He had never married and had no children, but that day, fate brought him into the life of a little girl. She was sitting on a bench, her eyes red and swollen from crying.

Kafka knelt beside her. "What's wrong?" he asked gently.

"I lost my doll," she sobbed.

Kafka looked around, but the doll was nowhere to be found. After a moment of silence, he said softly, "Don't worry. Come back tomorrow. We'll look again."

The next day, the girl returned, hopeful but nervous. They searched once more, but the doll was still missing. Seeing her disappointment, Kafka handed her a letter.

"It's from your doll," he said with a smile.

The girl's eyes widened as she unfolded the letter. In careful handwriting, the doll had written:

"Please don't cry. I've gone on a trip to see the world. I'll write to you about my adventures."

The girl's tears stopped, replaced by wonder. And so, a beautiful story began.

Day after day, Kafka met the girl in the park, each time with a new letter. The doll wrote of magical places and exciting journeys. She described the people she met and the lessons she learned along the way.

The little girl hung on every word. Kafka's vivid imagination brought the doll's adventures to life, making her absence feel less painful.

Eventually, the letters told of the doll's return to Berlin. One day, Kafka gave the girl a new doll.

"This doesn't look like my doll," she said, studying it carefully.

Kafka handed her another letter.

"My travels have changed me," it read.

The girl hugged the new doll tightly, accepting it with the same love she had for the original.

A year later, Kafka passed away.

Many years went by, and the little girl grew into a woman. One day, while sorting through old belongings, she noticed something tucked inside a tiny crevice of the doll. It was a small letter, delicate with age.

Her hands trembled as she opened it. The words inside, written by Kafka himself, read:

"Everything you love is very likely to be lost, but in the end, love will return in another form. Embrace the change. It is inevitable for growth."

Tears filled her eyes, but her heart was full.

Kafka's final message had come when she needed it most, reminding her that love never truly disappears—it simply transforms.

Narrative Context: This story is adapted from an anecdote about Franz Kafka, often shared as an inspiring tale of compassion and change. While not a direct excerpt from his works, the anecdote has been adapted from accounts and interpretations commonly associated with Kafka's life and legacy.

The Judoka With One Arm

A young man wandered into a Judo school one afternoon, eager to learn how to throw people—you know, for self-defence. But there was one problem. He had only one arm.

The sensei, noticing his disability, didn't let him join the regular classes. Instead, he kept the young man on the sidelines, making him practice a single beginner throw over and over.

Every day, while the other students practiced advanced moves and flashy sweeps, the young judoka repeated the same basic throw. Again, and again. Frustration built up.

After weeks of monotony, the young man couldn't hold it in any longer.

"I want to join the advanced class! Stop holding me back just because I'm different!" he blurted out.

The sensei paused, his face calm but serious. Then, he did something unexpected.

"Alright," he said, loud enough for the class to hear. "You'll fight everyone in the gym today. Let's see who throws who."

Nervous but determined, the young man stepped onto the mat. His stomach churned as he squared off against his first opponent. The fight began, and within seconds...THUD!

The sound of his opponent's back hitting the mat echoed across the room. The young man blinked in shock. Victory.

Match after match, the same thing happened. Each time a new opponent challenged him; he effortlessly threw them down using that same basic move.

After five straight wins, the young man stood stunned, his mind racing. How was this even possible? He turned toward his sensei, his eyes full of questions.

The sensei, as calm as ever, gave a small smile and said,

"The only known counter to that throw… is to grab the arm you don't have."

The realization hit him like a wave. His limitation had become his greatest advantage. Limitation can be a gift, if you allow it to be.

———◆◆———

Narrative Context: This story, often shared as an inspiring tale in martial arts circles, belongs to a long-standing tradition of moral stories that transcend borders and time. Though its origins are anonymous and believed to be in the public domain, this version has been adapted with fresh narration to suit today's reader

The Uneducated Surgeon

Cape Town university holds a prestigious place in the world of medicine. It was here that the first heart transplant was performed. One morning in 2003, Professor David Dent, a globally renowned surgeon, stood before a packed auditorium and made an unexpected announcement.

"Today, we honour the man who has trained more surgeons than anyone in the world. He is an extraordinary teacher and an exceptional surgeon, despite never having studied medical science formally." The audience erupted in applause as the professor took the name Hamilton. It was the largest standing ovation the university had ever witnessed.

Hamilton was born in Sanitani, a small village in Cape Town. His parents were shepherds, and he grew up herding goats, wearing goatskin, and walking barefoot in the mountains. When his father fell ill, young Hamilton left his village and moved to Cape Town in search of work.

At that time, construction was underway at the University of Cape Town. Hamilton joined the workforce as a labourer. He sent whatever money he could to his family, surviving on meagre meals and sleeping in open fields. Once construction was completed, he took up a job mowing the tennis court grass. For three years, he performed this task with unwavering dedication.

One warm morning, Professor Robert Joyce, who was conducting research on giraffes, needed help. He was studying why giraffes don't experience seizures when they bend their necks to drink water. During surgery on a giraffe, the animal kept shaking its head. A strong man was needed to hold the giraffe's neck steady.

Hamilton happened to be mowing the lawn nearby. Noticing his strong build, the professor called him in. Hamilton held the giraffe's neck for eight hours while the doctors took breaks for tea and coffee. When the operation was over, Hamilton quietly returned to mowing the lawn.

The next day, the professor called him again for assistance, and soon it became routine. Hamilton stood by, holding the giraffe's neck during multiple surgeries without complaint. Impressed by his patience and dedication, Professor Joyce promoted Hamilton to lab assistant.

As a lab assistant, Hamilton began assisting surgeons in the operating theatre. His understanding of the human body grew rapidly. His natural skill and steady hands gained the attention of senior doctors. By 1958, when Dr. Christiaan Barnard joined the university and began performing heart transplants, Hamilton had advanced from an assistant to an essential part of the surgical team.

His precision in stitching wounds was unmatched. His fingers moved with such finesse that surgeons entrusted him with teaching junior doctors how to suture. Over time, Hamilton became an integral figure at the university, earning the admiration of both students and senior faculty.

In 1970, Hamilton identified a liver artery that significantly simplified liver transplants.

Today, every successful liver transplant owes its success, in part, to Hamilton's discovery.

For 50 years, Hamilton was a fixture at the university. He would enter the operating theatre at precisely six o'clock every morning. People would often set their watches by his punctuality. Though he never had formal education in medicine, Hamilton trained over 30,000 surgeons during his lifetime. He was the first unlettered teacher of medical science and the first self-taught surgeon to achieve such acclaim.

When Hamilton passed away in 2005, he was buried on the university grounds. Even today, graduates take a picture by his grave before stepping into their professional lives.

Hamilton's remarkable journey began with a single yes. On the day he was asked to hold the giraffe's neck, he could have refused, claiming it wasn't his job. But his willingness to embrace the unexpected, opened doors he never imagined.

There are lot of unemployed people because they just look for a job, not for work! But Hamilton discovered the power of work. He proved that dedication and sincerity can transform ordinary labour into extraordinary achievements. His story teaches us that opportunities often lie where we least expect them.

———◆◆———

Narrative Context: Though the precise historical details of Hamilton's life may not be fully verifiable, this story has been adapted to enhance its narrative impact.

The Muddy Water

Once Buddha was traveling with his disciples when they passed by a serene lake. Feeling thirsty, Buddha said to one of his disciples, "I am thirsty. Could you please get me some water from the lake?"

The disciple walked to the lake, but just as he approached, a bullock cart crossed through it, churning up mud and making the water murky. He hesitated, thinking, how can I give this muddy water to Buddha? He returned and said, "Master, the water is too muddy. It's not fit to drink."

Buddha smiled gently but did not say anything.

After about half an hour, Buddha asked the same disciple to try again. The disciple went back but found that the water was still unclear. He returned, disappointed, and informed Buddha once more.

Some time passed, and Buddha asked him to go again. This time, when the disciple reached the lake, he saw that the mud had settled. The water was now crystal clear. He filled a pot and brought it back.

Buddha took the pot, looked at the water, and then turned to the disciple. With a calm smile, he said, "See what happened? You didn't stir the water or try to clean it. You simply waited, and the mud settled on its own. The water became clear effortlessly."

He paused, letting the words sink in, then added, "Your mind works the same way. When it is disturbed, just let it be. Give it time. It will calm down on its own. Having 'Peace of Mind' is not a strenuous job. It is an effortless process. Give it time! Peace comes naturally when you allow things to settle."

The disciple listened; his heart filled with understanding. The lesson was simple, yet profound.

Narrative Context: This story is adapted from ancient Buddhist teachings and has been shared in various forms to convey the importance of inner peace and patience.

Burned Biscuits

When I was a kid, my mom sometimes made dinner after a long, exhausting day at work. I remember one evening vividly. She placed a plate of eggs, sausage, and—much to my surprise—burned biscuits in front of my dad. I waited, curious to see how he would react.

Without missing a beat, Dad smiled, picked up a biscuit, and asked me about my day at school. I don't recall what I told him, but I do remember watching him smear butter and jelly on that charred biscuit. He ate every bite without a single grimace or complaint.

Later, as I left the table, I overheard Mom apologizing softly. "I'm so sorry about the burned biscuits," she murmured.

I'll never forget Dad's reply. "Honey, I love burned biscuits every now and then."

That night, when I went to say goodnight, I asked him if he really liked burned biscuits. He pulled me close, his arms warm and reassuring. "Your mom had a tough day, sweetheart. And besides," he whispered, "a little burned biscuit never hurt anyone."

As I've grown older, that moment has stayed with me. Life is full of imperfections—flawed moments, missed opportunities, and mistakes. I've forgotten birthdays, overlooked important dates, and stumbled more times than I can count. But over the years, I've realized that the secret to lasting relationships isn't perfection. It's about acceptance—embracing each other's flaws and celebrating differences.

This truth extends beyond marriage. It applies to friendships, parent-child relationships, and every bond we hold dear. Kindness, patience, and understanding build the foundation of meaningful connections.

So, the next time life serves you a burned biscuit, smile, and enjoy it. And remember— sometimes, it's not about the biscuit.

———◆◆———

Narrative Context: This story is adapted from an anonymous source and has been widely shared to highlight the importance of love, understanding, and acceptance in relationships. It draws upon themes rooted in public domain folklore and timeless moral storytelling.

The Race Of Integrity

Kenyan runner Abel Mutai was just a few feet from the finish line. But he misread the signage and slowed down, thinking the race was over. Spanish runner Ivan Fernandez was right behind him. Seeing the confusion, Ivan shouted at Mutai to keep going. But Mutai didn't understand Spanish.

In that moment, Ivan made a choice. He ran up behind Mutai and gently guided him forward, ensuring he crossed the finish line first.

After the race, a journalist asked Ivan, "Why did you do that? You could have won!" Ivan's expression was calm as he replied, "I didn't let him win. He was going to win. The race was his." The journalist, still puzzled, pressed further, "But you were right there. You had the chance!" Ivan's gaze was steady. "But what honour would there be in that victory? What would that medal mean?"

Winning is thrilling, no doubt. But winning does not always mean being first! If you are really going to do something in life, the secret is learning how to lose."

Narrative Context: This story is adapted from widely circulated accounts of the sportsmanship displayed by Ivan Fernandez during a cross-country race.

Ford And Mazda

Ford opened a state-of-the-art automatic transmission assembly plant in Batavia, Ohio. The plant was built around a simple philosophy: "Ford has good designs. Everything produced in this plant will conform to those designs." By that standard, the launch was a huge success. Every part, from the smallest component to the final assembly, met the design specifications perfectly.

But soon, a challenge emerged. Ford Escorts were selling so well worldwide that the Batavia plant couldn't keep up. To meet demand, Ford outsourced production to Mazda. The Japanese manufacturer received Ford's designs and began producing transmissions for Ford cars.

Months later, troubling data surfaced. Transmissions from Batavia had a repair frequency five times higher than those from Mazda. Warranty costs for Batavia's units were also significantly higher.

Perplexed, Ford engineers launched an investigation. They disassembled both Batavia and Mazda transmissions, measuring every detail—valve size, bore dimensions, sub-assembly, and final assembly. To their surprise, everything matched the specifications. Yet, Mazda's transmissions were far superior.

The reason? Mazda's engineers understood that quality goes beyond meeting specifications. While Ford engineers followed the blueprints, Mazda's team focused on minimizing variations around the nominal values. They didn't just meet the standard—they exceeded it. Their goal was excellence, not mere compliance.

The difference was in mindset. Ford's team operated with a compliance mentality—if it met the specifications, it was good enough. Mazda's team, however, saw conformity as a baseline, not the goal. They refined every process and component, ensuring the highest possible quality.

Compliance meets expectations. Quality exceeds them. Should we strive for quality, or conformity? The choice is ours.

———◆◆———

Narrative Context: This story is adapted from accounts of Ford's experience with outsourced transmission manufacturing. It should be considered as an illustrative anecdote rather than a documented historical event.

The Cycle Race

I was cycling this morning when I noticed someone about half a kilometre ahead. He was riding a little slower than me, which gave me a quiet sense of satisfaction. I thought, why not catch up with him?

So, I picked up my pace. Every few blocks, I was closing the gap. I pushed harder, my legs pumping faster, my heart pounding. Soon, I was only a hundred feet behind. Determined to pass him, I gave it my all. And finally... I did it! I zoomed past him, feeling a surge of victory.

But then it hit me—he didn't even know we were racing. He was just riding at his own pace, unaware that I had been locked in an imaginary competition. As I slowed down, I realized I had missed my turn. In my haste, I had ignored the beauty around me—the lush greenery, the cool breeze, the quiet calm of the morning. Worse still, my foot had slipped off the pedal twice, and I was lucky I hadn't landed on the sidewalk with a broken limb.

That's when a deeper truth struck me. Isn't this what happens in life? We get so caught up in competing with others—trying to outshine coworkers, impress neighbours, or prove ourselves to family and friends—that we lose sight of our own path. We chase after someone else's idea of success, only to realize we've veered far from where we were meant to go.

The problem with unhealthy competition is that it never ends. There's always someone with a better job, a bigger house, a nicer car, or more recognition. No matter how much we achieve, there's always someone ahead. But true fulfilment comes when you stop comparing. When you focus on your own journey, you discover peace and purpose.

Some people stay restless because they're too busy watching others—what they wear, where they go, or what they own. But life isn't a race where we all chase the same finish line. There

is no competition in Destiny. Each has his own.
Run your own Race.

Narrative Context: This story is an adapted version of a widely circulated tale, often shared in motivational and self-development contexts. Various versions exist, and its exact origin remains unclear.

The Ball Doesn't Know How Old I Am

A champion on and off the court, Martina Navratilova is more than a tennis legend. She is a symbol of resilience, honesty, and relentless drive. Widely regarded as one of the greatest tennis players ever, Martina's career spanned an incredible four decades. Her record is unmatched—59 Grand Slam titles and 9 Wimbledon singles championships. Against all odds, she became not only a sporting icon but also an inspiring leader.

Once, Martina was asked how she managed to stay focused, maintain her fitness, and keep her game sharp at 43. With a humble smile, she replied, "The ball doesn't know how old I am." Her words spoke volumes. The real game, she implied, isn't played on the court. It happens in the 6-inch space between your ears—your mind.

We don't truly live in bungalows, duplexes, or apartments. We live in our minds. And life feels wonderful when that space is clean and uncluttered. But when hatred grows on the table, regrets pile up in the corners, expectations boil over in the kitchen, and worries litter the floor, this real home becomes chaotic. Secrets get stuffed under the carpet, and the mess takes over.

The secret to performing well—on the court or in life—is managing the quality of your internal dialogue. What you say to yourself matters. The mind can be your greatest ally or your biggest enemy. When it's clouded with doubt, fear, and unnecessary noise, even great potential gets lost.

You need to stop yourself from stopping yourself. Performance is potential minus internal interference.

———◆◆———

Narrative Context: This story is adapted from various sources highlighting the life and achievements of Martina Navratilova.

The Thief's Story

At a wedding, a young man spotted his primary school teacher. Filled with respect and admiration, he approached him and said, "Do you remember me, Sir?"

The teacher smiled but shook his head. "I'm sorry, I don't. Please remind me."

"I was your student in 5th grade," the young man said softly. "I'm the one who stole a classmate's watch."

The teacher's expression remained calm as the young man continued.

"One of the boys had a beautiful watch, and I couldn't resist. I stole it. When he came to you crying, you asked us all to stand while you searched our pockets. I was terrified. I knew

I'd be exposed, labelled a thief, and shamed forever. But then…"

His voice caught for a moment. "You asked us to turn around and close our eyes. You searched every pocket. When you found the watch in mine, you didn't say a word. You just kept searching until you finished. Then you returned the watch without revealing the thief. You saved me that day."

The teacher listened quietly; his expression unchanged.

"You never mentioned it to anyone," the young man said, his voice filled with gratitude. "Not to the class, not to the other teachers. You protected my dignity and gave me a chance to change."

The teacher's eyes softened. He placed a gentle hand on the young man's shoulder and said, "I don't remember who stole the watch."

The young man blinked, surprised.

"I searched with my eyes closed," the teacher explained. "I didn't want to know."

For a moment, there was silence between them.

"*Education needs wisdom,*" the teacher finally said. We should always calculate the consequences of our actions. Protecting and reforming is tougher than exposing and expelling. Teaching isn't just about knowledge. It's about shaping individuals!

Narrative Context: This story is adapted from widely shared anecdotal sources reflecting similar narratives of empathy and wisdom in education.

Bowl Of Noodles

When I was a child, I was selfish and always grabbed the best for myself. I never thought it was wrong. When others distanced themselves, I blamed them instead of looking inward.

One day, my father cooked two bowls of noodles. One had an egg on top, and the other didn't. He smiled and said, "Choose the one you want, my child." Eggs were a rare treat in those days, something we only had during festivals. Without hesitation, I chose the bowl with the egg. As I ate, I felt proud of my decision. But when my father lifted his noodles, I was stunned—two eggs lay hidden beneath! I regretted my choice, but my father just smiled and said, "What you see isn't always the truth.

If you're too eager to take advantage, you might lose more than you gain."

The next day, he cooked noodles again—one bowl with an egg on top and the other without. He asked me to choose. Remembering my mistake, I picked the bowl without the egg this time. But when I reached the bottom, there was no egg at all! My father smiled once more. "Life can be unpredictable," he said gently. "Don't rely too much on past experiences. Sometimes, life plays tricks. Learn to adapt and stay calm."

On the third day, he prepared the same two bowls. But this time, I said, "Dad, you choose first. You are the head of the family and do so much for us." He didn't refuse and took the bowl with the egg. I expected nothing in mine. But as I dug deeper, I found not one, but two eggs!

My father's eyes were full of warmth as he said, "When you think of others first, good things naturally follow. When you trust your parents, they will always choose what's best for you."

These three lessons stayed with me. I've carried them through life and business. And true enough, success followed.

———◆◆———

Narrative Context: This story is a retelling of a widely known tale that appears in different versions across cultures and traditions. It is inspired by enduring themes found in public domain folklore and classic moral narratives.

The Happy Old Lady

The elderly woman, gracefully dressed with her hair neatly arranged, was a vision of elegance. At over 90, she still took great pride in her appearance. She and her husband had shared a beautiful life for 70 years. But after his passing, with no children or family to care for her, she chose to move to a nursing home. Even on the day she left her home for good, she looked radiant, her spirit undimmed.

When she arrived at the nursing home, she waited patiently in the lobby for hours until her room was ready. An attendant finally escorted her and described the small space she would now call home. "I love it!" the woman said, her eyes lighting up with the excitement of a child receiving a new puppy.

The attendant smiled but looked puzzled. "Mrs. Jones, you haven't even seen the room yet. Just wait," she said gently.

The lady responded softly but firmly, "My happiness doesn't depend on how the furniture is arranged. It depends on how I arrange my mind."

She paused for a moment, her eyes twinkling as she continued, "Happiness is a choice. I've already decided to love my room, the people around me, and my life. Every morning when I wake up, I make that decision. I can lie in bed thinking about the pain and what no longer works in my body, or I can get up and be thankful for what still does. Each day is a gift. As long as my eyes open, I will focus on today and the beautiful memories I've stored in my mind, ready for moments like this."

The attendant stood there; mouth slightly open, astonished by the woman's unwavering positivity. To anyone else, her life might have seemed filled with loneliness and loss. Yet, she radiated hope and grace.

"You see," the elderly woman continued, her voice filled with warmth, "problems happen automatically. Happiness, however, is a choice.

Hatred comes easily. Love takes intention. Negativity is effortless. But a positive attitude? That's a conscious decision. Complaining is easy. Gratitude, though? That's something we choose."

The attendant left the room that day, carrying not just admiration for the elderly lady but also a powerful reminder. Life is a series of choices. Choose wisely and live well.

— ❖ —

Narrative Context: This adaptation is rooted in folklore and collective wisdom passed down over centuries. While its exact origin remains uncertain, the story continues to teach meaningful lessons

The Burning House

A man returned to his town after a long trip, only to find his beloved house engulfed in flames. It was one of the most beautiful homes in the area, a source of pride and joy. Many had offered double its value, but he had refused to sell. Now, as he watched helplessly, the fire consumed everything he had cherished. His heart sank.

Just then, his eldest son ran up, whispering urgently, "Father, don't worry! I sold the house yesterday for three times its value. The deal was too good to pass up. Please forgive me for not waiting."

The father's eyes widened. "Thank God," he murmured, a wave of relief washing over him. His sorrow vanished, and he stood there, calm and detached, watching the fire like any other bystander. The house was gone, but it no longer belonged to him.

Moments later, his second son came rushing. "Father! Why are you standing there? Our house is burning, and you're smiling?"

"Don't you know?" the father replied, his voice steady. "Your brother sold it. It's no longer ours."

The second son's face turned pale. "We've only taken an advance," he said anxiously. "The buyer hasn't paid the full amount. I'm not sure he'll go through with it now."

The father's smile faded. His heart pounded, and panic gripped him once again. Tears welled up as attachment returned, dragging him back to sorrow.

Then the third son arrived, his face bright with news. "Father, relax," he said. "The buyer is a man of his word. I just spoke to him. He said it doesn't matter if the house is burnt. He's going to honour the deal and pay the full price."

In an instant, relief swept over the father again. His smile returned, and he stood once more as an indifferent spectator.

Nothing had really changed—the house was still burning. But the shift between attachment and detachment had altered everything.

This story paints a vivid picture of how our emotions are tied to ownership and attachment. When something belongs to us, its loss brings sorrow. But when we detach ourselves, we experience freedom. Happiness and sadness often stem not from events, but from how we perceive them. By learning to control our thoughts and direct them wisely, we can rise above unnecessary sorrow and navigate life with clarity and peace.

Narrative Context: This story is adapted from popular folklore with no definite origin or verifiable source, emphasizing the philosophy of detachment, often referenced in Eastern spiritual teachings.

The Old Car

When his daughter graduated high school, the father beamed with pride. "I'm so proud of you," he said. "You'll soon be heading out on your own. But before that, I have a gift for you. Come with me."

He led her to the garage and flipped a switch she had never noticed before. A dim light flickered on, revealing an old, dusty car tucked away in the corner. The car looked worn out, its paint faded, and wheels coated in grime.

The father handed her a set of keys and said, "I bought this car many years ago. It's old now, but it's yours. I just have one request. Take it to the used car lot and see how much they'll offer."

The daughter, though a little disappointed, took the keys and drove to the lot. When she returned, her expression said it all. "Dad, they only offered $1,000. They said the car's too rough."

"Hmm," he murmured. "Alright. Try the pawnshop next and see what they'll give."

She sighed, clearly unimpressed, but followed his wish. When she returned, her frustration was obvious. "They barely offered $100," she said. "They said it's too old to be of any value."

The father smiled gently. "One last try," he said. "Take it to the car club and show it to the members there."

By now, she was losing patience. But out of respect for her father, she agreed. When she came back, her face was radiant with disbelief.

"Dad! Five people offered me $100,0000 on the spot!" she exclaimed. "They said it's a Porsche 356 Speedster! A classic! Every collector there wanted it."

The father's eyes twinkled. "You see, my dear," he said softly, "if you aren't being valued, you're simply in the wrong place. Don't be angry. Don't be bitter. "The right place with the right people will always treat you the way you deserve to be. Know your worth and never settle where you're not appreciated. Never stay where people don't value you. The right place, with the right people, will always recognize your worth."

The daughter never sold the car. And she never forgot her father's words.

———◆◆———

Narrative Context: This narrative draws from a story that appears in various forms across cultures and traditions. It is widely circulated in the public domain in different formats across social media platforms.

The Missing Goat

It all began one lazy Sunday afternoon in a small town near Toronto, Canada.

Two mischievous schoolboys came up with a wild idea. They rounded up three goats from the neighbourhood and painted numbers on their sides—1, 2, and 4. Late that night, they snuck into their school and set the goats loose.

The next morning, chaos erupted.

As the school staff entered, the unmistakable smell of trouble greeted them. Goat droppings scattered near the entrance and along the stairs confirmed their fears. It didn't take long to find the three goats. But there was a problem.

Where was goat number 3?

The staff launched a frantic search. Teachers, helpers, security guards, even the canteen staff, all scoured every corner of the building. Hours passed, but goat number 3 was nowhere to be found. The mystery deepened. Concern turned into obsession. Classes were cancelled, and the search continued.

But goat number 3 didn't exist.

The boys had cleverly skipped that number, setting everyone on a wild goose chase—or in this case, a goat chase!

Isn't life often like that?

We get so caught up chasing things that don't exist—perfect relationships, flawless careers, or constant happiness. We focus on what's missing and forget to appreciate what's already there. The search for "goat number 3" drains our energy, steals our joy, and blinds us to life's blessings.

Stop chasing what isn't real.

Enjoy what's already yours. Don't let the non-existent imaginary goat number 3 waste your time, energy and happiness. Enjoy life with what you have.

Narrative Context: This narrative is an adaptation of a story found in multiple versions across different cultures and traditions. It reflects enduring themes from folklore and universally shared moral lessons that have long existed in the public domain.

The Invisible Labels

A car ahead crawled like a turtle, refusing to give way despite my constant honking. My frustration boiled as I edged closer, ready to lose my cool. Then, I noticed a small sticker on the rear window: "Physically challenged. Please be patient."

Everything shifted in an instant. My anger dissolved, and I slowed down, feeling a surge of protectiveness for the driver. I reached work a few minutes late, but it didn't matter.

That moment lingered in my mind. Would I have been patient if there had been no sticker? Why do we need labels to show empathy? What if people wore invisible labels on their foreheads? Labels like...

"Lost my job."

"Fighting cancer."

"Going through a painful divorce."

"Suffering emotional abuse."

"Grieving a loved one."

"Feeling worthless."

"Financially broken."

Everyone is fighting a battle we can't see. The least we can do is be kind, patient, and compassionate. We don't need visible labels to show understanding. Let's learn to respect the invisible ones.

———— ✦✦ ————

Narrative Context: This story is often shared in motivational circles and social media. While its exact origin remains unknown, this version has been adapted to highlight the importance of understanding others beyond what we can see.

Fox Or The Hedgehog

If you had to choose between being a fox or a hedgehog, which would you pick? Many would choose the fox—sleek, cunning, and quick. The hedgehog, small and slow, hardly seems impressive. But when it comes to success, being a hedgehog can make all the difference.

This idea comes from an ancient Greek parable: "The fox knows many things, but the hedgehog knows one big thing." The fox tries countless tricks to catch the hedgehog—sneaking, pouncing, and even playing dead. Yet, every time, the hedgehog curls into a spiky ball, leaving the fox with a stinging nose. Despite its cleverness, the fox never realizes the hedgehog masters one thing perfectly—defence.

Philosopher Isaiah Berlin explored this concept in his 1953 essay, *"The Hedgehog and the Fox."* He divided people into two types: foxes and hedgehogs. Foxes chase multiple goals, spreading their efforts thin. Their scattered focus leaves them achieving little. Hedgehogs, however, simplify life. They focus on one powerful idea and pursue it relentlessly, leading to greater success.

Business researcher Jim Collins expanded on this idea in his 2001 classic, *"Good to Great."* He introduced *The Hedgehog Concept*—the idea that individuals and organizations thrive when they identify what they do best and devote all their energy to it. Collins found that when times get tough, those who focus on their strengths, like hedgehogs, are the ones who survive and succeed.

Research backs this up. Studies show that focusing on strengths leads to faster growth than trying to fix weaknesses. People who play to their strengths also tend to be happier, less stressed, and more confident. The lesson is clear: Find your strength, focus on it and pursue it with unwavering focus. Like the hedgehog, doing one thing well can lead to extraordinary success.

Narrative Context: This story has been adapted from multiple sources, including the works of Isaiah Berlin and Jim Collins.

The Mayonnaise Jar

Some stories never get old. This is one of them. When life feels overwhelming, remember the lesson of the mayonnaise jar and the two cups of coffee.

A philosophy professor stood before his class, a few items on the table. Without a word, he picked up a large, empty mayonnaise jar and filled it with golf balls. He asked the students if the jar was full. They nodded, agreeing it was.

Next, he poured a box of pebbles into the jar. He gave it a gentle shake, and the pebbles settled into the spaces between the golf balls. Again, he asked if the jar was full. The students agreed it was.

Then, the professor took a box of sand and poured it in. The sand filled the remaining gaps.

Once more, he asked if the jar was full. This time, the students answered with a confident "yes."

Finally, he pulled out two cups of coffee and poured them into the jar. The liquid seeped into the spaces left between the grains of sand. The class burst into laughter.

When the laughter died down, the professor spoke. "This jar represents your life," he began. "The golf balls are the most important things—family, health, friends, and passions. If everything else was gone, but these remained, your life would still be full."

"The pebbles are the other things that matter—your job, house, and car. The sand is the small stuff. If you pour the sand first, there's no room for the golf balls or pebbles. The same goes for life. Focus on what truly matters. The rest is just sand."

He paused, then added, "Take care of the golf balls. Spend time with your loved ones. Go for that checkup. Take your partner out for dinner. There will always be time to clean the house and fix the leaky faucet."

A student raised her hand. "What about the coffee?" she asked with a smile.

The professor grinned. "Ah, I'm glad you asked. No matter how full your life feels, there's always room for coffee with friends"

———◆◆———

Narrative Context: This timeless tale is widely shared in motivational talks and classrooms. The origin of this story is unclear. This version has been adapted for clarity and modern relevance.

Zohnerism

In 1997, 14-year-old Nathan Zohner presented a project at his school science fair titled Dihydrogen Monoxide: The Unrecognized Killer. His goal? To warn people about a dangerous and deadly chemical known as DHMO.

Nathan's report highlighted alarming facts:

- DHMO can cause severe burns in both its gaseous and solid forms.

- It's a major component of acid rain and is often found in cancerous tumours.

- It accelerates corrosion of metals and natural elements.

- Ingesting excessive amounts leads to sweating, urination, and potential death from water intoxication.

- Withdrawal from DHMO is always fatal for those dependent on it.

After presenting these facts, Nathan asked 50 classmates whether DHMO should be banned from school. An overwhelming 43 students—a staggering 86%—voted to ban it immediately.

But here's the twist: Dihydrogen monoxide is just water.

Nathan's experiment, "How Gullible Are We?" exposed a powerful truth—facts can be manipulated to deceive. Life throws us challenges, and we often misread situations or misunderstand others. But when facts mislead us, that's on us.

A closer look at the name reveals the truth. "Di" means two, "hydrogen" is self-explanatory, "mono" means one, and "oxide" refers to oxygen. Two hydrogens, one oxygen. H_2O. Water.

When Nathan conducted this experiment in 1997, smartphones didn't exist. But chemistry classes did. His classmates could have asked a teacher or taken a moment to think critically. But they didn't.

When it is hard to be right, there is nothing wrong with being wrong. But if we let facts deceive us, that is on us. Today, we have the world's knowledge at our fingertips. Any information is just seconds away. Yet, we still get "zohnered" more often than we'd like to admit. It's easy to twist facts and lead people wherever the manipulator wants.

The solution? Stay alert. Think critically. Verify before you believe. Don't be deceived by selective information. The truth is usually simpler than it seems.

——◆◆——

Narrative Context: This story is adapted from the real-life experiment conducted by Nathan Zohner in 1997, known as 'How Gullible Are We?"'

The Curacao Bridge

In 1888, a bridge was built in Curaçao to connect two parts of the city. To maintain it, officials proposed a toll. But they wanted it to be "progressive"—the rich would pay, and the poor could cross for free.

The question was: How do you tell who's rich and who's poor? Their solution was simple. Rich people wore shoes. Poor people didn't. So, they introduced a rule—if you crossed the bridge wearing shoes, you paid a tax. If you were barefoot, you crossed for free.

It seemed like a brilliant, foolproof plan. But it failed.

Wealthy people simply took off their shoes and walked barefoot. Meanwhile, the poor, too proud to be seen as poor, borrowed shoes just to cross. The system collapsed.

What does this teach us?

- Poverty is often hidden in plain sight.
- Poverty is more in the mind!
- The rich stay rich by spending less. The poor often stay poor by spending more.
- Human behaviour is rarely rational.
- The wealthy have access to better financial advice.
- Taxing the rich to help the poor sounds noble but is rarely straightforward.

Now, ask yourself: Are you "borrowing shoes" to cross any bridges in your life? If so, maybe it's time to stop.

———— ◆◆ ————

Narrative Context: This story is adapted from historical accounts of the Curaçao bridge toll system of 1888.

Big John Doesn't Pay

One morning, a bus driver started his usual route. Everything was going smoothly. A few passengers got on, a few got off. Nothing out of the ordinary.

But at the next stop, a giant of a man stepped onto the bus. He was six feet eight, built like a wrestler, with arms that seemed to hang down to his knees. He glared at the driver and growled, "Big John doesn't pay!" Then, without another word, he marched to the back and sat down.

The driver, barely five feet three and thin as a rake, didn't argue. He wasn't about to pick a fight with a man who looked like he could bench-press the bus. But the incident bothered him. The next day, Big John did the same thing.

And the day after that. Every day, Big John got on, refused to pay, and took his seat.

The driver couldn't take it anymore. He started losing sleep, haunted by thoughts of Big John. Finally, he decided to do something about it.

Determined to stand up for himself, he enrolled in bodybuilding classes. He learned karate, judo, and self-defence. By the end of summer, he was stronger, more confident, and ready to take on Big John.

Monday came. Big John climbed aboard as usual, stared at the driver, and said, "Big John doesn't pay!"

But this time, the driver didn't cower. He stood up, flexed his muscles, and glared right back. "And why not?" he demanded.

Big John blinked, looking genuinely surprised. "Big John has a bus pass," he said calmly.

The driver stood there, stunned. All that worry, all those sleepless nights, and the solution had been right in front of him all along.

Be sure to identify the problem clearly before working hard to solve it. Most solutions are simple. We complicate the issues.

Confront your problems early, don't lose sleep over them.

———◆◆———

Narrative Context: This story is adapted from various versions of the 'Big John Bus Pass' anecdote.

Duck or Eagle

Are you a Duck or an Eagle? Ducks quack and complain. Eagles soar above the crowd. Ever wondered which one you are? Harvey Mackay, a renowned author and speaker, shared an eye-opening experience.

While waiting for a cab at the airport, Harvey was surprised when a spotless taxi pulled up. The driver, dressed in a crisp white shirt, black tie, and pressed black slacks, stepped out and opened the door for him.

"Good morning! I'm Wally, your driver," he said with a smile, handing Harvey a laminated card. "While I load your bags, please read my mission statement."

Harvey, slightly taken aback, read the card: "Wally's Mission: To get my customers to their destination safely, quickly, and affordably, all while providing a friendly environment.''

Harvey was impressed. The inside of the cab was just as spotless as the outside. As Wally slid into the driver's seat, he asked, ''Would you like a cup of coffee? I have regular and decaf in thermoses.''

Harvey, thinking it was a joke, said, ''No thanks, I prefer soft drinks.''

To his amazement, Wally replied, ''No problem. I've got regular and Diet Coke, water, and orange juice in the cooler.''

Harvey, now completely floored, asked for a Diet Coke. As they drove off, Wally handed him another laminated card. ''Here's a list of radio stations and the type of music they play. Let me know if you'd like to listen to something.''

As they approached Harvey's destination, Wally explained the best route for that time of day. He even offered to chat about the sights or let Harvey enjoy the ride in peace.

Curious, Harvey finally asked, ''Wally, have you always treated your customers this way?''

Wally smiled in the rear-view mirror. ''No, not always,'' he admitted. ''For the first five years, I was just like every other cabbie—complaining, quacking like a duck. Then, one day, I heard Wayne Dyer on the radio. He said, 'Stop complaining! Differentiate yourself from the crowd. Don't be a duck. Be an eagle.'"

"That hit me hard," Wally continued. "I realized I was quacking, not soaring. So, I made a choice. I decided to change. I looked around, saw how other cabbies worked, and figured out how to be different. I started with small changes. When my customers appreciated them, I added more."

Harvey asked, "Did it make a difference?"

"Oh, absolutely!" Wally beamed. "In my first year as an eagle, I doubled my income. This year, I'll probably quadruple it. I don't wait at cabstands anymore. My customers call me directly or leave messages on my cell. If I can't make it, I send a reliable driver and take a cut. It's been life-changing!"

Wally transformed himself by refusing to settle for being ordinary. He chose to stand out, to be exceptional. And it paid off. You might think that a perfect application of the story would be regarding providing outstanding customer service. In fact, that is one perfect application. But, in looking a little deeper we find life-success truths that lead to living a more meaningful and abundant life.

1. Success Begins with Choice

   Wally made a conscious decision to change. He took responsibility for his life and chose to be an eagle.

2. Start Small but Start

   Big changes often begin with small steps. Wally didn't overhaul everything overnight. He started where he was and gradually improved.

3. First Impressions Matter

   Like it or not, people judge within seconds. Wally's clean cab and professional attire made a lasting impression.

4. Attitude + Action = Altitude

   Wally didn't just think about being different. He acted on it. His positive attitude, combined with action, lifted him above the rest.

5. Reap What You Sow

   Wally invested in excellence and reaped the rewards. If you want success, you need to plant seeds of effort and improvement.

So, what about you?

Are you soaring like an eagle or still quacking like a duck? It's never too late to choose to fly.

Narrative Context: This story is adapted from Harvey Mackay's original account of Wally the cab driver, shared in his motivational writings and speeches.

A Bridge To Nowhere

Honduras, Central America, is home to the Choluteca Bridge, a 484-meter marvel stretching over the river Choluteca. Known for its storms and hurricanes, the region demanded a structure that could withstand nature's fury.

In 1996, a Japanese firm was tasked with building this new bridge. They delivered a masterpiece—sturdy, resilient, and ready for anything Mother Nature could throw its way. By 1998, the bridge was open to the public. People marvelled at the design and applauded the brilliance behind its construction.

Then came Hurricane Mitch in October of the same year. It unleashed 75 inches of rain in just four days—the kind of downpour that would normally fall over six months. Chaos followed. The Choluteca River swelled, flooding everything in its path. Thousands of lives were lost. Every bridge in Honduras was destroyed.

Every bridge, except one.

The Choluteca Bridge stood firm, untouched by the hurricane's wrath. But there was a problem. The bridge had survived, but the landscape had not. The roads leading to and from the bridge had vanished. Worse still, the raging floods forced the river to carve a new path. When the waters receded, the river no longer flowed under the bridge. It now ran alongside it.

A bridge to nowhere. Strong. Impressive. But completely useless.

That was many years ago. But the message of the Choluteca Bridge is more relevant today than ever.

We often focus on building the perfect solution, the strongest product, or the most advanced service. We refine and polish our skills, mastering one domain after another. Yet, we forget one crucial thing—the problem itself might change.

Look at your career. You might be investing time and money to become an expert in a specific niche. But what if that expertise becomes obsolete? Before renovating that office or expanding branches, ask yourself—will physical office spaces still matter tomorrow?

The world is changing faster than ever. Technologies evolve. Markets shift. Needs disappear. We build the strongest bridges but forget that rivers can change course.

Adaptation matters more than strength. Built to last may sound inspiring, but built to adapt is what truly ensures survival.

So, the next time you admire a picture of a grand structure—perhaps even the Choluteca Bridge—let it remind you of one thing. It's not about building something that lasts forever. It's about building something that can change when the world around it changes.

Otherwise, you may be left with a marvel.

A superb bridge.

Over nothing.

To nowhere.

—◆◆—

Narrative Context: This story is adapted from the widely shared account of the Choluteca Bridge and its lessons on adaptability.

The Bamboo

The legendary cricketer Rahul Dravid, known for his calm and steady approach, was once asked by a fan why he didn't play aggressive, stormy cricket. Dravid smiled and replied with a story—a story about patience, discipline, and long-term success.

He spoke about the Chinese bamboo plant. When its seed is planted, nothing happens for the first five years. No shoots, no sign of growth, no visible change. Yet, beneath the surface, the bamboo is working hard, quietly developing a strong root system. It prepares itself to handle the tremendous growth that will come. Then, in the sixth year, something incredible happens. The bamboo shoots up, growing almost 90 feet in just a few weeks.

But did the bamboo grow 90 feet in a few weeks? No. It grew over five years and a few weeks. Without that long, silent preparation, the rapid growth would have been impossible. Those five years, seemingly without results, were as much a part of the growth process as the visible spurt that followed.

Life works the same way. Whether it's building a career, mastering a skill, or achieving success, the initial phase often feels unrewarding. Effort seems futile. Results are invisible. But just like the bamboo, this invisible phase is laying the foundation. It's the time when we develop resilience, discipline, and strength. Without it, sustainable success is impossible.

Dravid's own career echoed this principle. He built his reputation not with flashy strokes, but with unwavering focus, endless practice, and relentless patience. Each inning he played was like the bamboo, growing stronger with every passing moment.

Success doesn't come overnight. There are no shortcuts. Good days bring joy, while bad days teach valuable lessons. Both are essential to life. Keep going. Don't quit.

Narrative context: While the exact origin and authenticity of this story cannot be definitively verified, it is adapted from widely shared anecdotes about Rahul Dravid and the story of the Chinese bamboo.

The Kings Highway

Once upon a time, a king built a grand highway for his people. Before opening it, he announced a challenge: whoever travelled the road best would receive a box of gold.

On the day of the contest, people arrived in style. Some rode in elegant chariots, dressed in fine clothes, and carried luxurious food. Others laced up their sturdiest shoes, eager to prove their endurance. They all set off, determined to impress the king.

As they journeyed, many grumbled about a large pile of rocks and debris that blocked part of the road. It slowed them down, dirtied their clothes, and frustrated their travels. One by one, they reached the end, each complaining to the king about the obstacle.

Late in the day, a lone traveller arrived, exhausted and covered in dust. He bowed before the king and placed a small chest of gold at his feet. "I found this under the pile of rocks," he said. "Someone must have lost it."

The king smiled. "That gold is yours."

The man's eyes widened. "Mine? But I've never owned such wealth."

"You have now," the king replied. "For the one who travels best is the one who makes the road better for those who follow."

———◆◆———

Narrative Context: Loosely adapted from a traditional narrative commonly shared in motivational literature.

Not Everything That Counts
Can Be Counted

During World War II, fighter planes returning from combat missions were riddled with bullet holes. To prevent more planes from being shot down, Air Force officers decided to add armour. But there was a problem—too much armour would make the planes heavy and sluggish, while too little wouldn't provide enough protection. The challenge was to find the right balance. But where should the armour go?

Mathematicians and engineers were brought in to analyse the damage. They mapped bullet holes per square foot and discovered a pattern. Planes had 1.93 bullet holes per square foot near the tail and only 1.11 bullet holes per square foot near the engine. The officers believed the solution was obvious—add extra armour where the bullet holes were most concentrated, around the tail.

Then Abraham Wald, a brilliant mathematician, stepped in with a surprising insight. "You're looking at this the wrong way," he said. "These planes returned safely despite the damage. The planes that didn't return likely took hits in places you don't see—like the engine." Wald explained that planes hit in the engine never made it back, which is why there were fewer holes in that area on surviving aircraft. His logic was simple but profound: protect the areas that had fewer visible bullet holes, because those were the places where damage was fatal.

He gave another example to make his point clear. "If you visit a hospital's recovery ward, you'll see more patients with bullet wounds in their arms and legs than in their chests. That's not because people don't get shot in the chest—it's because those who do often don't survive to make it to the hospital."

Wald's insight changed the Air Force's approach. They reinforced the engines, giving planes a better chance of making it home.

His analysis illustrated a crucial truth—what you don't see can often be more important than what's visible.

As Albert Einstein once said, "Not everything that counts can be counted, and not everything that can be counted, counts."

---✦✦---

Narrative Context: Adapted from the story of Abraham Wald and his work on survivorship bias during World War

The Krauss Maffei Story

It was 1946. Germany lay in ruins, devastated by the aftermath of World War II. The Allies had emerged victorious, but cities like Munich bore the scars of relentless bombings by the British Royal Air Force. Amidst this grim backdrop, a group of dignified men stood at the Munich railway station, awaiting guests from India. They were the directors of Krauss Maffei, a prestigious German engineering company known for its expertise in locomotive manufacturing. But now, the company was in shambles, struggling to survive in the post-war wreckage.

A train pulled into the station. Stepping off were the Indian guests—directors from the Tata Group. Among them was J.R.D. Tata, the young, tall, and composed chairman. The Tata delegation had come to discuss the possibility of manufacturing locomotives in India. What they encountered, however, was not a thriving engineering giant but a city reduced to rubble and a company desperately seeking hope.

The German hosts had an unusual request. They asked the Tata directors to take some of their unemployed engineers to India, along with their families, and provide them with jobs and shelter. "They are skilled people," the Krauss Maffei directors explained. "They will do whatever you ask them. They can also teach your people." There was no formal contract involved—India was still under British rule, and engaging with German corporations was strictly prohibited. But this was not about contracts. It was about trust and survival.

The Tata directors agreed. They assured the Germans that the engineers would be well taken care of. Soon, a group of German engineers from Krauss Maffei arrived in India. Tata Motors welcomed them with open arms, providing housing, security, and meaningful work. These engineers went on to make invaluable contributions to Tata Motors, sharing their expertise and transforming the company's technological capabilities.

Years passed. Germany recovered, rising from the ashes of war. The Krauss Maffei company, too, regained its stature. Then, one day, the directors of Krauss Maffei received a letter from India. It was from Tata Group. The letter expressed heartfelt gratitude for the contributions of the German engineers and, surprisingly, provided compensation for the knowledge and skills they had imparted.

The Germans were stunned. There had been no contractual obligation. The Tata Group had done a great service by giving the engineers a new life during the war's darkest days. Why, then, this unexpected gesture? The offer came as a complete surprise.

Few years later, another remarkable chapter unfolded. Tata Motors needed to provide a legally binding financial guarantee to the German government for a new project. But the German government regulations complicated the process. When the matter was referred to German bankers, they had a simple response: "A guarantee on Tata's letterhead, signed by the chairman, is more valuable than any banker's guarantee."

What led the Tata directors to send that letter of compensation to Krauss Maffei? Perhaps they had no clear answer themselves. But they did it because it was the right thing to do. Doing the right thing isn't always about adhering to formal agreements or meeting external expectations. It's about living up to one's own standards of fairness and trust.

The story of Krauss Maffei and Tata is not just about engineering or business. It's a timeless reminder that integrity transcends contracts. We always know, if we listen deeply enough to our inner voice, whether we are being totally fair and right. The Krauss Maffei story holds such a beautiful lesson for all of us.

———◆◆———

Narrative Context: Although the exact sequence of happenings may not be verifiable, this story is adapted from multiple sources, including historical accounts of the collaboration between Tata Group and Krauss Maffei.

The Story Of Defeat

Some of the most unforgettable moments in sports aren't about victories or records. They are about humanity, fair play, and the spirit of sportsmanship. This is one such story—how JRD Tata, the longest-serving Chairman of the Tata Group, lost a race but gained a lifelong friend.

In 1930, the Aga Khan announced a prize for the first Indian to fly solo between India and England. The journey had to be completed within six weeks of commencement, and the prize was open for a year. Three Indians accepted the challenge. But fate had a special plan for two of them—JRD Tata and Aspy Engineer. Their paths crossed unexpectedly in Egypt, changing the course of their lives.

JRD Tata, holder of India's first-ever flying license numbered '1', set off from Karachi in a Gipsy Moth plane. Aspy Engineer, a young Parsi from Karachi, flew in the opposite direction, starting from London. As JRD later recalled:

"I was 26, and Aspy was just 19. A young, enthusiastic Parsi boy from a modest family in Karachi. I flew to Cairo, but my compass was 45 degrees off, which threw me off course. It was a Sunday, and the British Air Force was closed, so I had to go to Alexandria. That's where I saw another little Moth. I wondered— what's it doing here? And it was Aspy!"

JRD's curiosity led him to approach Aspy.

"What are you doing here?" I asked. He said, 'I'm waiting for spark plugs.' His spark plugs had failed, and without them, he was stranded. I was shocked. 'Don't tell me you left England without spare plugs!' He admitted he had, but he had ordered replacements. I wasn't going to let him wait and lose his chance. I had spare plugs, so I gave them to him. He gave me his Mae West (life jacket) in return. We parted ways. Aspy reached Karachi just two-and-a-half hours before I landed in Paris. He won the race."

Aspy claimed the prize. When asked if he regretted losing by such a narrow margin, JRD's response was heartfelt.

"This is something anybody would have done. That's what sport is about. If you don't have sportsmanship, what's the point?"

Aspy's victory opened new doors. He was admitted to the fledgling Indian Air Force and later became India's second Chief of Air Staff after independence. JRD, on the other hand, went on to pioneer India's civil aviation industry, establishing Tata Airlines in 1932, which later became Air India.

Years later, both men had carved remarkable legacies in Indian aviation, but the real triumph lay in their enduring friendship.

The mark of a true sportsperson is not just about how well you play the game, but equally about how you play the game; it's not just about how you win, but also about how you lose.

———•❖•———

Narrative Context: While the precise details may not be verifiable, this story is adapted from multiple historical accounts of JRD Tata's aviation journey and his association with Aspy Engine

Cows Don't Give Milk

A peasant used to tell his children when they were young, "When you turn 12, I will share the secret of life." The eldest waited eagerly. When he finally turned 12, he asked his father about the secret.

The father nodded, but with a serious expression, said, "I will tell you, but promise not to share it with your brothers yet."

He leaned in and whispered, "The cow doesn't give milk."

The boy blinked, confused. "What do you mean?"

His father smiled gently. "Exactly what I said. The cow doesn't just give milk. You have to wake up at 4 in the morning, walk through the muddy corral, tie the cow's tail, hobble her legs, sit on a stool, place the bucket, and do the work yourself. Only then do you get milk."

The boy listened in silence as his father continued. "That's the secret of life, son. If you don't milk the cow, you don't get milk. But too many people today think that cows give milk automatically. They believe life is as simple as wishing, asking, and receiving. But no, life doesn't work that way."

His voice grew firm. "Happiness? You earn it. Success? You work for it. Nothing comes easy. Without effort, all you'll find is frustration."

The father locked his son in the eye. "Remember this well. The government, your parents, or your charming looks aren't going to hand you everything. Cows don't give milk, son. You have to work for it."

———✦✦———

Narrative Context: This story is an adapted version of a tale that exists in various forms across cultures and traditions. It draws upon themes rooted in public domain folklore and timeless moral storytelling

Quantity Leads To Quality

On the first day of class, Jerry Uelsmann, a photography professor at the University of Florida, divided his students into two groups. The left side of the classroom was placed in the "quantity" group. Their grade would depend solely on the number of photos they produced. A hundred photos meant an A, ninety a B, eighty a C, and so on.

The right side, however, was in the "quality" group. They only needed to submit one photo for the entire semester, but it had to be flawless to earn an A.

As the semester unfolded, something unexpected happened. When the final photos were reviewed, the best ones came from the quantity group. These students had spent the term capturing hundreds of photos.

They experimented with different angles, adjusted lighting, and explored various techniques in the darkroom. Each mistake taught them something new. With every click of the shutter, they refined their craft.

In contrast, the quality group spent most of their time theorizing about perfection. They analysed, speculated, and aimed for an ideal image. But with little practice, they ended up producing a single, mediocre photo.

The outcome was clear. The students who focused on quantity, who showed up regularly and embraced trial and error, unknowingly achieved quality.

In the end, practice beat perfection. Quantity leads to quality.

Narrative Context: This story is adapted from an experiment conducted by Jerry Uelsmann, highlighting the importance of consistent effort in mastering a craft.

The Styrofoam Cup

A former Under-secretary of Defence was once invited to speak at a prestigious conference. As he stood on the stage, delivering his prepared remarks and PowerPoint presentation, he took a sip from his Styrofoam cup. Pausing, he smiled and went off script.

"Last year," he began, "I spoke at this same conference. But back then, I was still the Undersecretary. They flew me business class. Someone met me at the airport and escorted me to my hotel, where check-in was already taken care of. The next morning, I was greeted in the lobby and driven to this venue. I entered through the back entrance, was guided to the green room, and handed a steaming cup of coffee in a beautiful ceramic cup."

He glanced at the Styrofoam cup in his hand and continued, "This year, I'm no longer the Undersecretary. I flew economy class. I took a taxi to the hotel and checked myself in. There was no one waiting for me in the lobby. This morning, I took another taxi, walked through the front entrance, and found my way backstage. When I asked for coffee, someone pointed me to a machine in the corner. I poured this cup myself."

He paused for a moment and said softly, "The ceramic cup was never meant for me. It was for the position I held. I deserve this Styrofoam cup."

His words carried a profound truth. As you climb higher in life, gaining fame, fortune, and power, people treat you differently. Doors open effortlessly. Someone offers you a drink before you even ask. You are addressed with titles of respect, showered with gifts, and surrounded by admiration. But none of it is truly for you. It's for the position you occupy.

Time doesn't stand still. One day, those perks fade, and what remains is just the person you are—the one who deserves a Styrofoam cup. The lesson is clear: enjoy the privileges that come with your position but never forget to be humble and grateful. Because in the end, it's not the cup that matters, but how you carry it.

———◆◆———

Narrative Context: Adapted from a widely shared story available in the public domain. Various versions of this narrative exist, and while its exact origin is unclear, it has been recounted in different forms for its powerful message and impact."

The Large Tree Branch

A young girl and her father were walking along a quiet forest path. Birds chirped softly in the background as sunlight filtered through the leaves. Suddenly, they came across a large tree branch blocking their way.

"Do you think i can move it if I try?" the girl asked, her eyes filled with determination.

Her father smiled and said, "I'm sure you can, if you use all your strength."

The girl bent down and pushed with all her might. She strained and struggled, but the branch wouldn't budge. Disappointed, she looked up and said, "You were wrong, Dad. I can't move it."

Her father gently urged, "Try again, using all your strength."

She took a deep breath and pushed harder. Her small hands gripped the branch tighter, but despite her effort, the branch remained firmly in place. Frustrated, she sighed, "Dad, I really can't do it."

Her father knelt beside her, his voice calm but firm. "Sweetheart," he said softly, "I told you to use *all* your strength. But you didn't."

She looked at him, confused.

"You didn't ask for my help," he said, placing a reassuring hand on her shoulder.

The girl's eyes widened as she realized what he meant.

Real strength doesn't come from doing everything alone. It lies in knowing when to seek help. No one possesses all the strength, wisdom, or resources to succeed entirely on their own. Asking for support isn't a sign of weakness—it's a sign of understanding that we thrive through interdependence.

Narrative Context: This narrative has been adapted from a story attributed to an anonymous source, frequently found in motivational literature. Multiple variations of the story exist in the public domain, and its precise origin remains unverified

Coffee, Egg Or Potato

One time, a young girl poured out her frustrations to her father. Life felt overwhelming, filled with endless setbacks. She was tired of struggling. Her father, a chef, listened patiently and then led her to the kitchen.

He placed three identical pots on the stove and filled them with equal amounts of water. He lit the flame and waited silently as the water heated. When it began to boil, he added ground coffee beans to one pot, eggs to another, and potatoes to the third. The girl stood by, watching with growing impatience, wondering what her father was trying to show her.

After twenty minutes, he turned off the heat. He carefully spooned the potatoes into a bowl, placed the eggs in another, and poured the coffee into a mug. Turning to his daughter, he asked, "What do you see?"

"Potatoes, eggs, and coffee," she replied, confused.

"Look closer," he said gently. "Touch the potatoes."

She pressed her fingers into the soft, tender flesh.

"Now, break an egg."

She cracked the shell, revealing a firm, hard-boiled egg.

"Finally, taste the coffee."

The aroma made her smile as she sipped the rich, flavourful brew.

Her curiosity finally got the better of her. "Dad, what does this mean?"

He looked at her and said softly, "All three faced the same challenge—boiling water. But each reacted differently. The potato went in strong and unyielding, but the heat softened it. The egg, fragile with its thin shell, grew hard on the inside. But the coffee... it was different. It transformed the water, turning the very thing that caused its stress into something better."

He paused, letting the words sink in. "When life throws problems at you, which one will you be?"

Narrative Context: Adapted from a popular motivational story of non-verifiable origin, widely circulated in the public domain.

The One Percent Rule

The fate of British Cycling changed dramatically in 2003. The organization, which governed professional cycling in Great Britain, had struggled for over a century. Since 1908, British riders had won just one Olympic gold medal. Worse, no British cyclist had ever claimed victory in the Tour de France.

Their performance was so poor that a top European bike manufacturer refused to sell bikes to the team. They feared that associating their brand with the British riders would hurt sales.

Then came Dave Brailsford. Hired as the new performance director, he introduced a strategy that would change everything. His philosophy was simple yet powerful—"the aggregation of marginal gains." He believed that if you improved every aspect of cycling by just 1 percent, the accumulated results would be extraordinary.

"If you break down everything involved in riding a bike and make tiny improvements everywhere," Brailsford explained, "you'll see a significant change when you put them all together."

Brailsford and his team started with the basics. They redesigned the bike seats for comfort and rubbed alcohol on the tires to improve grip. Riders wore heated over-shorts to maintain optimal muscle temperature, and biofeedback sensors tracked individual responses to different workouts. But they didn't stop there.

They looked for improvements in unexpected places. They tested various massage gels to speed up muscle recovery and hired a surgeon to teach the team how to wash their hands properly to avoid catching colds. They even customized pillows and mattresses for better sleep and painted the inside of the team's truck white to spot dust that could interfere with bike performance.

These small changes, combined with relentless dedication, led to results beyond imagination. Between 2007 and 2017, British cyclists won 178 world championships, 66 Olympic and Paralympic gold medals, and five Tour de France titles. It was the most successful run in cycling history.

But how did a team of ordinary athletes transform into world champions? The secret lay in those small, consistent improvements. Tiny changes may seem insignificant at first, but over time, they create remarkable results.

We often overestimate the impact of one defining moment and underestimate the power of small daily improvements. Whether it's losing weight, building a business, or mastering a skill, we assume massive success requires massive effort. But real success comes from small disciplines practiced consistently.

A 1 percent improvement every day may not seem like much, but over a year, it compounds to make you 37 times better. On the flip side, small errors in judgment, repeated daily, can lead to failure.

You may never find yourself racing in the Tour de France, but the concept of marginal gains applies to all aspects of life. There's immense power in small improvements and steady progress. So, where are the 1 percent gains waiting to be discovered in your life?

Narrative Context: This story is adapted from an excerpt in James Clear's Atomic Habits.

Karoly Takacs

Karoly Takacs was a proud member of the Hungarian army and a phenomenal pistol shooter. By 1936, he was considered one of the best in the world. But there was one problem—he was only a sergeant. Since Hungary allowed only commissioned officers to participate in the Olympics, Takacs was denied a chance to compete.

Soon after the event, the rules changed, giving Takacs the opportunity to chase his Olympic dream. He was the favourite to win gold in the 1940 Tokyo Olympics. Fuelled by hope and ambition, he trained relentlessly, determined to bring home victory.

But fate had other plans. In 1938, during a routine army training session, a faulty grenade exploded in his hand. His right hand—his shooting hand—was shattered beyond repair. Takacs was devastated. His dreams of Olympic gold seemed to go up in smoke. He spent a month in the hospital, not only nursing his wounds but also mourning the loss of his future in the sport.

When he was discharged, Takacs disappeared from the public eye. Months passed in solitude, but he wasn't giving up. Unknown to the world, he was training in secret. His mind refused to dwell on what he had lost. Instead, he asked himself—"What can I do with what I have?"

In the spring of 1939, the Hungarian National Pistol Championship was held. To everyone's surprise, Takacs showed up. Fellow shooters welcomed him, offering sympathy for his loss. They assumed he was there as a spectator, eager to relive the thrill of competition.

But Takacs had other plans. When his turn came, he stepped up and picked up the pistol—with his left hand. The crowd watched in stunned silence. One shot. Then another. Shot after shot, each hitting the bullseye. Their disbelief turned into awe as Takacs not only competed but won the championship.

The secret was out. While others had written him off, Takacs had taught himself to shoot with his non-dominant hand. Months of silent dedication had brought him back to the top.

But his Olympic dream was delayed once again. The 1940 Olympics were cancelled due to World War II. Takacs waited patiently for another chance. The 1944 Olympics were cancelled too. Yet, he held on. He refused to hang up his boots.

By 1948, Takacs was 38. Many believed he was too old to compete at an elite level. But Takacs wasn't ready to fade away. At the London Olympics, he not only proved his critics wrong but also set a world record in the rapid-fire pistol event, clinching the gold medal. His moment had finally arrived. He stepped onto the podium, a gold medal around his neck and a quiet smile of victory on his face.

Four years later, Takacs did it again. He won another gold in the 1952 Olympics, solidifying his place as one of the greatest marksmen in history. His relentless pursuit of excellence earned him a place in the Olympic Heroes list of the International Olympic Committee.

Most shooters would have given up after losing their dominant hand. But not Takacs. He didn't dwell on what he had lost. He focused on what he could control and mastered a new skill against all odds. Life doesn't always go as planned. Circumstances change, and challenges arise. But Takacs showed the world that it's not about how hard you can hit—it's about how much you can take and keep moving forward.

Karoly Takacs ended his career as the legend who never gave up.

Narrative Context: This story is adapted from historical accounts of Karoly Takacs' life and achievements.

Empty Your Cup

The Empty Your Cup story is a famous one that is retold in Zen circles time and time again. It was also one of the iconic Bruce Lee's favourite stories, so it's definitely worth knowing about.

A learned man once visited a Zen teacher to inquire about Zen. As the teacher spoke, the man frequently interrupted, offering his own opinions. He had a comment for everything. The teacher listened patiently but said nothing.

After a while, the teacher decided to make tea. He poured the tea into the visitor's cup. He kept pouring even after the cup was full, letting the tea overflow onto the table. The learned man watched in shock. "Stop!" he exclaimed. "The cup is full. No more will fit."

The teacher smiled. "Like this cup," he said softly, "you are full of your own opinions. How can I teach you anything unless you first empty your cup?"

The message was clear. When your mind is too full of assumptions, opinions, and beliefs, there's no space for new ideas to enter. It's a trap many people fall into, especially those striving to improve themselves. They consume information endlessly, filling their minds to the brim. They believe they know enough and don't need to learn more. But that's an illusion.

No one can ever know everything—not about the world, not about others, not even about themselves. That's why a dose of humility is essential. You need to empty your cup every day. Only then can you make space for new experiences, fresh ideas, and different perspectives.

It's not about blindly accepting everything poured into your cup. Sometimes, you need to let things sit, reflect on them, and pour out what doesn't serve you. But if your cup is always full, nothing new can enter.

When you engage in conversations, do you listen with an empty cup, ready to learn? Or is your mind already crowded with opinions, like the learned man's? Emptying your cup means being open to life's lessons—because they're everywhere, waiting to be noticed.

Bruce Lee often spoke of this wisdom. He believed that "the usefulness of a cup is in its emptiness."

Empty your cup. Every. Single. Day.

Narrative Context: This story is adapted from a popular Zen parable, famously cited by Bruce Lee.

The Barbell Doesn't Care

One evening, Shreya came home looking annoyed and worn out. She dropped her bag on the floor, flopped on the sofa, and let out a loud sigh.

Her dad walked in with a cup of coffee and raised an eyebrow. "Rough day?"

"The worst," she mumbled. "Nothing goes right. I study, I try to be nice, I do everything, and still... life just doesn't play fair. I try so hard, and still things don't go my way. Other people don't even try, and everything works out for them." It's like I'm always swimming upstream."

He sat down next to her and took a sip of his coffee. "Hmm. Sounds familiar."

Shreya looked at him. "Seriously, Dad. I'm tired of trying so hard and getting nowhere. Some people just have it easy."

He nodded, took a deep breath, and spoke.

"Remember, Shreya, when you were small, and used to accompany me to the gym?" "And you used to try and lift the dumbbells and the kettlebells! Do you remember it?"

Shreya blinked. "Uh... are you trying to tell me to work out right now?"

He grinned. "No, just hear me out. The barbell, the dumbbell, the kettle bell, or for that matter any other gym equipment. They have important hidden lessons for us all."

She gave him a side-eye. "This better not be one of your weird life metaphors."

He chuckled. "It is. But it's a good one. The dumbbell or the barbell doesn't care who lifts it. It doesn't cheer you on. It won't feel bad for you if you're tired or had a bad day. It just sits there." It looks right in your face and says: "This is going to be hard, and it will take a lot of effort, but the payoff is awesome. Take it or leave it. It's your choice."

She tilted her head, a little curious now.

"But here's the thing," he continued. "If you pick it up, and you show up every day, no matter what, you get stronger. Slowly. But surely. If you don't, it just stays right there. No judgment. No reward either."

Shreya thought a bit, and said "So... it's like life?"

"Exactly," Dad said. "Life's not unfair. It's just neutral. It's like a barbell. It gives you chances, but you've got to show up and do the work. No one's going to do it for you. And it's not going to hand things over just because you tried once." The opportunities are there, but it's on us to seize them and start grinding. It's all on us. Always has been. Always will be.

She was quiet for a second, then gave a small smile. "I guess the barbell's kind of savage."

He laughed. "Yeah. But it's also honest. And it works—if you do."

"Alright, lesson taken. Still not working out today though." She said.

He raised his cup in mock salute. "Fair enough. Tomorrow's a good day to start."

Narrative Context: This story, often shared in fitness circles, comes from a timeless tradition of moral tales that cross cultures and generations. Though its original author is unknown and believed to be in the public domain, this version has been freshly adapted to resonate with today's readers.